Welcome to Camp Santanoni and the Santanoni Preserve, all nestled within the Forest Preserve of the vast Adirondack Park. Built in the early 1890s, Santanoni was dedicated to the idea that the wild Adirondack Mountains were the perfect spot for humans to find respite from the clutter and noise of civilization. More than a hundred years later, visitors still enjoy the wonder of this Great Camp—the cool, summer breezes on the main lodge porch, the splendor of fall colors around Newcomb Lake, or the peace and solitude of a winter ski trip.

    The Department of Environmental Conservation and its partners have worked diligently to restore and preserve the historic fabric of Camp Santanoni for future generations. I encourage everyone to explore this historic gem. The lasting memories Santanoni bequeaths to those fortunate enough to experience its beauty are well worth the trip.

> Joe Martens, *Commissioner*
> New York State
> Department of Environmental Conservation

# Map of Santanoni Preserve

- Little Santanoni Mountain
- Wolf Pond Mountain
- Moose Pond
- Wolf Lake
- Moose Mountain
- Shaw Pond
- Ward Pond
- Santanoni Brook
- Baldwin Mountain
- Newcomb Lake
- Honeymoon Bridge
- Twin Bridges
- Service Complex
- Sucker Brook
- Farm Complex
- Duck Hole Bridge
- Main Camp Complex
- Santanoni Preserve Bridge
- Gate Lodge Complex
- Rich Lake
- Fishing Brook
- Duck Hole
- Lake Harris
- RT 28N
- NEWCOMB
- Hudson River
- Newcomb River

Santanoni Peak

# *Santanoni Preserve*

*It takes time to make a
comfortable place to live in
this great wilderness.
You cannot merely
buy land and
build a house.
A patient contest
with nature
is necessary . . .*

—Robert C. Pruyn, 1915

Robert Pruyn imagined a gentleman's estate; his wife, Anna, imagined a wilderness retreat. The Santanoni Preserve is a marriage of these two ideals of nature. In 1892 on the shore of Newcomb Lake, the Pruyns built a rustic log villa, the first element of an estate that would eventually include a model farm, service complex, and formal gate lodge surrounded by almost 13,000 acres of wild land. Girlhood summers in the southern Adirondacks had encouraged a love of nature in Anna, who preferred the woods to the social life of Albany. Though drawn to a more pastoral relationship with nature, Robert had a deep respect for its contemplative power, instilled during a formative trip to Japan as an adolescent. It was a Japanese aesthetic—a reverence for nature and an appreciation for rustic refinement—that bound the two ideals together in Camp Santanoni.

Banker, industrialist, civic leader—Robert Clarence Pruyn was typical of his generation and social class. But an opportunity to accompany his father to Japan when he was 14 set him apart. Born in 1847 in Albany into a prominent Dutch family that had made its money in the lumber and paper industries, he was the son of Robert Hewson Pruyn and Jane Anne Lansing. In 1862 Robert H. Pruyn became minister to Japan and took young Robert with him. Arriving at a time of great upheaval following the opening of the country to the west by Commodore Perry, Robert experienced a cultural aesthetic rooted in nature. Residing in a former temple exposed him to the principles guiding Japanese design. The experience would fuel a lifelong fascination with its art and culture.

After returning from the Orient, Pruyn's life resumed a conventional course. He attended Rutgers College, graduating in 1869. It was at Rutgers that he became friends with Robert H. Robertson, who as a prominent architect 25 years later would design the log villa at Santanoni. In 1873

*Courtesy Albany Institute of History and Art Library*

Robert Pruyn and Anna Martha Williams married; four children would follow between 1874 and 1881—Edward (Ned), Ruth, Robert, and Frederick (Fritz). He enjoyed a swift rise through the ranks of the National Commercial Bank in Albany, becoming president in 1885. For the next 46 years, he served at the helm of what is today Key Bank, one of the largest banks in the country. By the late 1880s, the Pruyns had amassed enough wealth to begin planning a country estate like families of similar social status. But rather than choosing a resort area like Newport, Rhode Island, or the Hudson River Valley, they chose Newcomb, New York, described in one publication as "the heart of the wilderness."

Though sparsely settled, the land that Robert Pruyn purchased was not virgin wilderness. By 1830 there were eight documented farms in Newcomb. About the same time, the discovery of iron ore deposits six miles northeast of Newcomb Lake spurred the establishment of the mining village of Adirondac, later called Tahawus. Although the mine closed in 1856, heirs to the ironworks leased land from the company in the 1870s to establish one of the first fish-and-game clubs in the Adirondacks with its own preserve, the Preston Ponds Club, later called the Adirondack Club. Robert Pruyn may well have hiked to nearby Newcomb Lake in the 1870s or 1880s with his friend Robert Robertson, a club member. In 1890 Pruyn purchased 6,500 acres of land that included the lake at a state tax sale in Albany. The process of stitching together the 22 parcels that would become the Santanoni Preserve had begun.

*This sequestered loch [Newcomb Lake] is one of the fairest waters of this lake-bespangled and leafy-solitude. It is crescent-shaped, island-adorned, and mountain-locked . . .*

— E.R. Wallace, *Descriptive Guide to the Adirondacks,* 1895

*The Pruyn family at Santanoni,* from left: *Ned, Robert C., Ruth, Robert D., and Fritz*
*Courtesy Adirondack Architectural Heritage*

    The Pruyns' desire to build an isolated retreat sprang from a changing attitude toward wilderness. Rather than an adversary to conquer, it became a refuge from the city for recreation and spiritual renewal. Sportsmen, attracted to the region by its romantic depiction in literature and art, brought word of its singular beauty back to urban centers. An improved railroad network opened the Adirondacks to tourism, transporting a growing middle class with more money and leisure time to hotels and resorts on the region's lakes. The rising popularity of the region as a tourist destination coincided with the early stirrings of a wilderness conservation movement both to preserve the natural beauty of the area for sportsmen and tourists and to protect business interests threatened by the impact of uncontrolled logging on important commercial waterways with headwaters in the Adirondacks. Private preserves offered a measure of protection to land within their boundaries and a way for the wealthy to avoid mixing with the middle class. The unique building type on these preserves became known as a "Great Camp" in the 1980s.

    Distinguished by its remote setting on a private lake, the Great Camp was a complex of buildings, constructed in a rustic style with natural materials for both functional and decorative elements. Though designed to harmonize with the surrounding landscape, some were, in fact, so extensive and elaborate that they dominated it instead. Because of their isolation, many operated as small villages with a farm, blacksmith shop, icehouse, and other supporting structures. Here, the wealthy could "rough it" with all the comforts of home.

    While the log villa at Camp Santanoni incorporates the basic elements of a Great Camp, the influence of a Japanese aesthetic created a plan that respects the contours,

*Rooftops at Zempukuji Temple,*
*U.S. Legation, Edo (Tokyo), 1862,*
*residence of the Pruyns from 1862 to 1863*
*Courtesy Albany Institute of History and Art Library*

colors, and textures of the surrounding forest more successfully than most other camps. The villa spreads across the landscape, following a low ridge above Newcomb Lake. The forest "comes to the very doors of the camp," according to the 1893 New York Forest Commission report. The estate was composed of four distinct areas: the main camp complex, the service complex, the farm complex, and the gate lodge complex. Each formed a visually cohesive group, united by a dark brown and earthy red color scheme. In all, about 50 buildings dotted the preserve at its peak.

Three designers shaped the character of the buildings at the Santanoni Preserve. Robert H. Robertson (1849-1919), a New York-based architect, designed the log villa in 1892. Best known for urban and suburban buildings in Victorian and Classical Revival styles, his design shows the influence of Robert Pruyn's interest in Japanese culture in its resemblance to a type of villa—a central lodge surrounded by individual buildings united by a single roof and covered porches. Agricultural designer Edward Burnett's expertise in scientific farming is evident at Santanoni's farm, where principles of efficiency, hygiene, and yield guided the building layout and design between 1902 and 1908. Another New York firm, classically trained Delano and Aldrich, was responsible for the gate lodge, creamery, and artist's studio between 1904 and 1905. The firm's use of a rustic stone arch in each building is a unifying visual element at the preserve.

*An outing at Moose Pond*

Robert and Anna Pruyn encouraged an active, outdoor lifestyle at Santanoni. Guests rose early to fish and returned to a lunchtime conversation dominated by reports on the morning's catch. Days filled with boating, hiking, swimming, and picnicking were followed by evenings with music, poetry composition, dancing, and games. The attentive care of a large service staff, from the guide who led the wilderness hikes to the laundress who washed muddy clothing afterward, made camp life feel simple and effortless to guests.

By the 1930s the rarefied lifestyle of Camp Santanoni was under threat. The stock market crash of 1929 and Robert Pruyn's failing health weakened the financial underpinnings of the family's use of the preserve. After Robert's death in 1934 and Anna's in 1939, younger generations continued to enjoy the magic of Santanoni, though in a much less formal way. Eventually, however, the Pruyn descendants could no longer afford the operational costs. In 1953 Crandall and Myron Melvin of Syracuse, New York, purchased the entire preserve, where their extended family gathered for nearly two decades. But their use was dramatically different—a reflection of changing times and social class. Although the Melvins enjoyed outdoor life there, they also spent much of their vacation time repairing buildings that the Pruyns had once hired staff to maintain. The tragic disappearance on the preserve of Melvin grandchild Douglas Legg in 1971—a mystery that remains unsolved—marked the end of Santanoni as a private family estate. In 1972 the Melvins sold the property to the newly created Adirondack chapter of the Nature Conservancy, which transferred it to the state of New York. Today, the Department of Environmental Conservation manages the site in partnership with Adirondack Architectural Heritage and with some financial support from the Town of Newcomb.

*The main camp from Newcomb Lake*

# Private Preserves and the Conservation Movement

Economic considerations provided a practical incentive for wilderness conservation in the Adirondacks. By the 1870s unregulated logging threatened the fragile balance between wilderness and human industry. Lumber and paper companies clear-cut large tracts of forest, then deliberately defaulted on taxes so ownership reverted to the counties. Lacking the financial resources or legislative power to manage this land, the state encouraged the formation of private preserves to protect the region's natural resources. Some wealthy individuals purchased land for family estates, others pooled funds to acquire land for fish-and-game clubs. Though founded to a certain extent on self-interest, these preserves made important contributions to the new fields of scientific forestry and wildlife management, whose goals were to maintain healthy forests and game populations for the enjoyment of tourists and sportsmen. Many preserve owners hired professional foresters to oversee selective timber harvesting for improved wildlife habitat and robust forest growth.

A hiking party at the Moose Pond boathouse

In fact, the state Forest Commission and United States Forest Service later adopted stewardship practices first employed on these preserves.

Although private preserves removed some land from exploitation, businessmen concerned about the impact of deforestation on the water quality and flow of the St. Lawrence, Hudson, and Mohawk rivers, as well as the Erie Canal—vital commercial waterways whose headwaters lay in the Adirondack Mountains—lobbied the state legislature to regulate logging practices. Sportsmen, worried about the impact of aggressive logging on game and fish populations, supported this effort. Their combined pressure on the government led to the establishment of the first state forest preserve in the country in 1885, mandated to preserve the land for watershed protection, wildlife conservation, and public recreation. Two other important pieces of conservation legislation followed in the next decade: establishment of the Adirondack Park in 1892 and passage in 1894 of Article XIV, the ground-breaking "Forever Wild" article of the state constitution, which required that all Forest Preserve lands remain "wild forest land" in perpetuity. Today, as the largest park in the lower 48 states, the Adirondack Park reflects this approach to land management, balancing economic development on private lands with wild land preservation on public lands.

The debate about wilderness conservation raged as Robert Pruyn began to develop his estate in the early 1890s. Camp Santanoni was built seven years after the establishment of the Forest Preserve and the same year as the creation of the Adirondack Park. Like his friend and Santanoni guest, Theodore Roosevelt, who as U.S. president made wilderness conservation a national priority, Pruyn embraced conservation as a way to manage natural resources for sustainable use in the future. He was a founding member of the Association for the Protection of the Adirondacks, established in 1902. For Robert Pruyn, it was: "The land, the land, always the land."

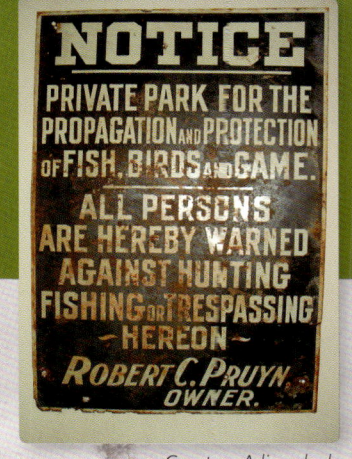

*Courtesy Adirondack Architectural Heritage*

# The Gate Lodge Complex

Trail Register
Trailhead Gate
Chicken Coop Site
West Cottage
Sheep Shed Site
Parking Area
Outhouse
Outhouse
DEC Operations Shop
Barn Site
Garage
Parking Area
Parking Area
12
Farmhouse Site
Camping Shelter Site
Boathouse
Gate Lodge
Lake Harris
Fishing Brook
Rich Lake
Santanoni Preserve Bridge

Site
Existing

N

An estate as vast as Camp Santanoni—with its farm, maple sugaring, off-season logging operation, and numerous recreational activities—required the skills of a professional manager. Robert Pruyn commissioned the gate lodge, the last major building on the preserve, to house Ellis Baker, who served as the preserve's superintendent from about 1907 to 1915, and his wife, Dillie, *(left)*. Prior to coming to Santanoni, Baker had been the accountant at the Jekyll Island Club, an exclusive island retreat off the coast of Georgia for some of the country's wealthiest families—the Pruyns included—at the turn of the century.

*Courtesy Adirondack Museum*

A traditional feature of the English country estate, the gate lodge had both a practical and symbolic purpose. Its presence announced the visitor's arrival at a prestigious estate, discouraged intruders, and provided housing for a caretaker and staff. Robert Pruyn hired the New York-based architectural firm of Delano and Aldrich to design the gate lodge. William Adams Delano (1874-1960), *right,* and Chester Holmes Aldrich (1871-1940) studied at Columbia University and the École des Beaux-Arts in Paris and apprenticed at the renowned firm of Carrère and Hastings. Though better known for classically inspired suburban and country estates than the rustic lodges favored in the Adirondacks, the firm's reputation for responding to the particular attributes of a site in its designs appealed to Pruyn's respect for the land.

*Courtesy the Columbiana Collection, Columbia University*

This approach is evident in the gate lodge, which captured a striking vista of Lake Harris and the mountains beyond through a massive stone arch. Living areas overlooked Fishing Brook between Harris and Rich lakes to take advantage of the restful sound of running water and the southern exposure. Five fireplaces of local fieldstone warmed the rooms. Six bedrooms on the second floor accommodated the superintendent's family and probably additional bachelor staff. The superintendent's office on the right and a tool room on the left flanked the arch. Like the farm buildings, the gate lodge was clad in dark brown cedar shingles to harmonize with the surrounding forest. The exposed truss work in the arch gables is a typical element of the Stick Style popular at the time.

Around 1915 the Pruyns' son Fritz and his family began to use the lodge as their primary summer residence. More comfortable than the main camp and closer to village amenities, it may have appealed to grandchildren restless for distraction. Though the upstairs bedrooms were cramped, Fritz's daughter, "Sis," remembers it as cozy. By 1930 only the office was in use. After the Melvins purchased the property in 1953, Crandall Melvin made it his family's residence. Though he renovated the interior, adding electricity and covering some of the plaster with plasterboard, he did not alter the original plan.

Visitors to Camp Santanoni crossed an elegant Pratt truss steel bridge, installed by Pruyn in 1893, and followed a winding road, bordered by a stone wall, through the stone arch of the gate lodge and past the farm to the main camp. The leisurely route allowed time to admire panoramic views of distant mountains to the east and the farm complex a mile away across open pastures now reclaimed by the forest.

Two farmhouses and a barn stood on the parcels that Robert Pruyn purchased in 1903 to build the gate lodge. A farmhouse to the north of the lodge was removed to improve the view, and the barn (ca. 1905), once located across the driveway from the garage, burned in 1992. Pruyn renovated the other farmhouse, located at the present-day trailhead, for staff housing. The West cottage, home of assistant gardener Walter West and his family from the mid-1920s to 1931 when the farm closed, fell into disrepair in the 1930s but was renovated around 1940 for Arthur Tummins, who was caretaker at Santanoni until retirement in 1976. Constructed sometime before 1876, its exterior trim, window arrangement, and framing differ from other buildings on the preserve, suggesting it existed prior to Pruyn's purchase of this parcel.

Other buildings at this end of the preserve included a boathouse on Lake Harris, probably constructed about 1915 when Fritz Pruyn's family began to use the gate lodge as their summer residence, a screened camping shelter, chicken coops, and a sheep shed, its occupants likely expected to trim the pastures for pastoral effect. The garage, added by the Melvins in the 1950s, incorporated salvaged timbers from Pruyn-era buildings.

# Edward Burnett and Scientific Farming

In the late 1800s and early 1900s, a growing interest in the application of science to agriculture gave rise to the field of agricultural science or "scientific farming." Here too, as they had in wilderness conservation, the wealthy had the financial resources and leisure to lead the effort. Private estates often had model farms that, though rarely profitable, introduced new practices and technology to improve hygiene, yield, and efficiency, much as scientific forestry sought to improve the health and yield of the forest.

*Courtesy NYSDEC*

A preeminent expert in scientific farming at the time was Edward Burnett (1849–1925). After graduating in 1871 from Harvard College, Burnett managed Deerfoot Farm, his father's property in Southborough, Massachusetts. Here he experimented with techniques to maximize milk production and processing and to improve hygiene through proper waste disposal, the separation of processing from milking areas, and the prevention of spoilage during transportation to market. Burnett improved the country's Guernsey dairy herd by importing stock to strengthen breeding lines and by customizing the care and feeding. He would apply what he learned at Deerfoot to future jobs.

From 1889 to 1892, Burnett developed and managed one of the earliest model farms in the country at Biltmore, the Asheville, North Carolina, estate of George Washington Vanderbilt. Here he built a reputation as an agriculturalist and developed a business planning and managing model farms. Around 1900 he established a practice as an agricultural architect in New York City and designed model farms throughout the Northeast. Between 1888 and 1903, Burnett was a regular speaker at the New York Farmers' Club on topics ranging from hay cultivation and farm buildings to cattle feeding and pig rearing. Though not a member of the so-called "Fifth Avenue Farmers," Robert Pruyn probably knew enough of Edward Burnett by reputation to hire him.

# The Farm Complex

Farm Manager's House

Icehouse/ Refrigeration Ruins

Creamery

Blacksmith Shop/ Garage Site

Sheep Shed Site

Barn Ruins

Piggery Ruins

Poultry House Ruins

Small Pigpen Site

Slaughterhouse Site

Duck House Ruins

*There is independence, delight and peace in the isolation, but everybody needs good food for health and it cannot be imported by tins . . .*

—Robert C. Pruyn, 1915

Shed Site

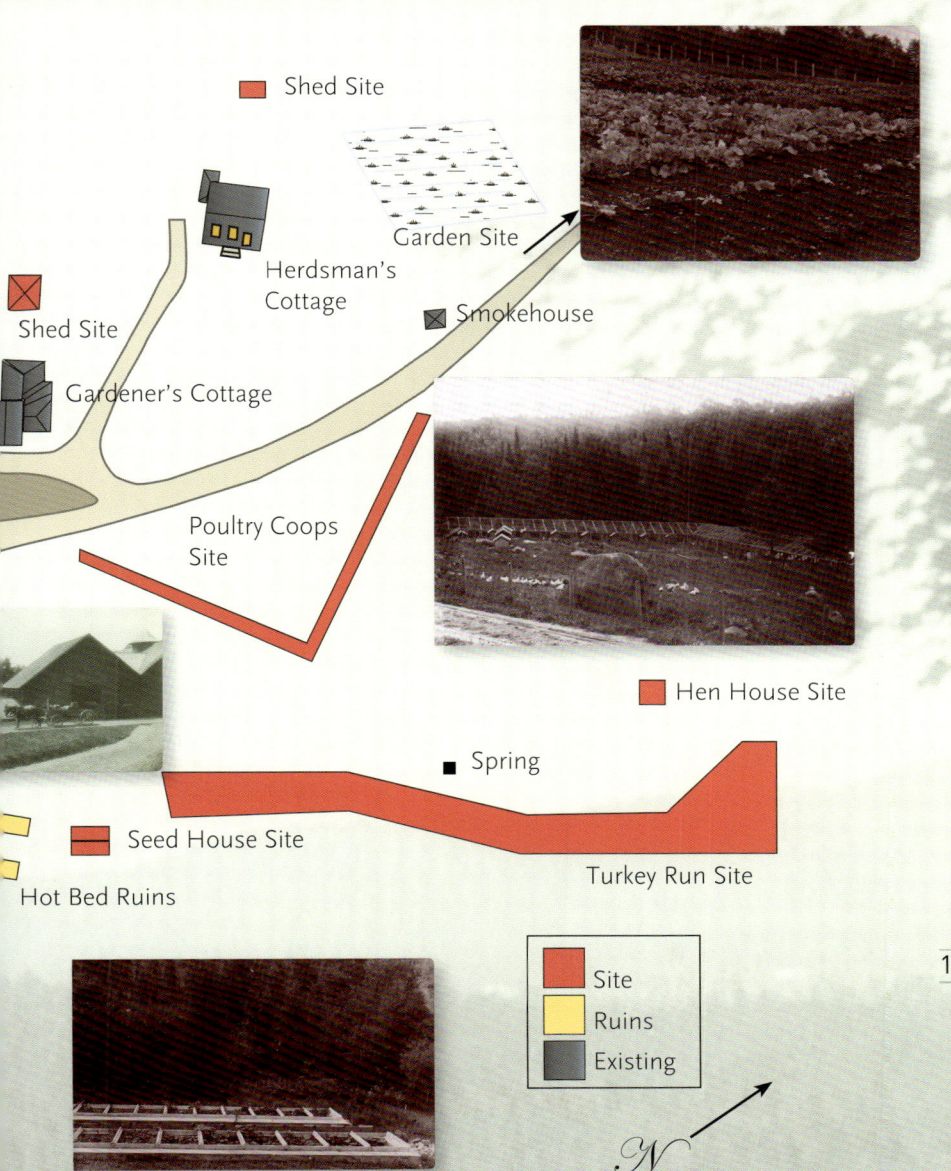

Herdsman's Cottage

Garden Site

Shed Site

Smokehouse

Gardener's Cottage

Poultry Coops Site

Hen House Site

Spring

Seed House Site

Turkey Run Site

Hot Bed Ruins

Site
Ruins
Existing

N

For Robert Pruyn, a model farm was both necessity and hobby. Local farms were scarce due to the region's harsh climate and densely forested, rocky terrain. Shipping food from distant urban markets was expensive and impractical. But necessity was not Pruyn's only motive; a model farm was an important element of the English-style country estate he sought to carve out of the Adirondack wilderness. Here he could apply the same competitiveness that brought him success in the business world to the development of a gentleman's farm, distinguished by its advanced technology, award-winning breeds, and high yields. It was what he called his "patient contest with nature," a place at once productive and picturesque.

Pruyn located his farm on an existing farmstead one mile north of the gate lodge and four miles south of the main camp, where pastureland and a timber-framed farmhouse already occupied a south-facing slope.

About 1895 he built a simple, multi-use barn for feed and equipment storage, cows and draft horses, and dairy operations. Riding and carriage horses were stabled farther up the road at the service complex.

By 1901 Pruyn was ready to plan a more extensive model farm. For this he hired the farm designer Edward Burnett. Between 1902 and 1908, the farm complex grew to include more than 20 buildings supporting the production and processing of a wide variety of vegetables, meat, poultry, dairy, and wool products. Though other Great Camps had farms, Santanoni's was one of the largest and most sophisticated at the time. It produced enough to supply the Pruyns' table at camp, with food to spare for their Albany home. In the off-season, caretaker Art Tummins made a weekly trip to Albany with chickens, eggs, vegetables, fruit, maple syrup and sugar, dairy products, smoked ham, bacon, spring water, and firewood.

Burnett oversaw the development of all aspects of the farm operation, from the design and layout of major buildings to integration of the most modern equipment to selection of breeds. No doubt he was adept at balancing his scientific approach to farm operation with Robert Pruyn's desire to create an attractive complex of buildings and livestock for his guests to admire.

*Courtesy Adirondack Architectural Heritage*

Modernizing the dairy operation was Edward Burnett's first project. In 1902 he expanded the 1895 barn, a traditional New England-style "bank barn," so-called because it was sited against a steep slope to allow access at road and cellar level. Hay, grain, and equipment were stored on the second and third floors and livestock in the cellar. Burnett added a similar bank barn to the west of the original barn to house milking and feeding operations and to stable the cows in the cellar and a hay mow on the second level; he converted the original into a horse barn. A sheltered concrete manure pit abutted the south side of the new barn. Also added at this time was an early example of the wooden stave silo, appearing before the practice of fermenting corn for winter feed was common. However, the silo quickly fell into disuse, as the short summers did not permit enough time for the fermentation process. The feed room at its base, lined with galvanized sheet iron to discourage rodents, remained in use. In 1904 a wagon shed was added at the far east end and an open cow shed at the far west end *(opposite page, upper left)*.

Sited on a gentle slope across from the barn complex, the creamery (1904) incorporated state-of-the-art equipment and technology for the sanitary processing and storage of dairy products. By the 1880s public health officials had identified contaminated dairy products as a possible cause of tuberculosis, but it took 40 more years

*Creamery and gardener's cottage (far right)*

for the government to require dairy operations to separate the storage and processing from the stabling areas. The creamery contained three rooms to accomplish this: the milk room, where the cream was separated; the washroom, where equipment could be sanitized with hot water; and the boiler room, which housed a furnace and hot water tanks. Farm workers carried five-gallon cans of milk from the barn to the milk room and poured it into cream-separator cans set in cold water piped continuously from a spring behind the building. The empty cans were sent to the washroom for sterilization and storage. Containers of milk, cream, and butter were kept chilled in an icehouse, later updated with refrigeration equipment, until needed at the main camp or in Albany. Unwanted buttermilk was poured into a tank, then piped underground to the piggery across the road, where it was drawn from a tap for slop.

With input from Edward Burnett on the creamery's location and plan, Delano and Aldrich, architects of the gate lodge, designed a picturesque counterbalance to the barn complex across the road. The creamery's massive fieldstone piers and arches *(below)* recall the arch at the gate

(Left) *Barnyard showing, from left: stone wall of piggery, poultry house, sheep shed, and barn complex*

Photo ©Jane Riley

lodge and artist's studio. The design incorporated features to keep the building cool, including thick masonry walls, interior secondary casement windows, and air ducts to vent the warm air. Concrete floors and plaster walls and ceilings were easy to clean.

Burnett arranged other major farm buildings below the barn complex to create an enclosed barnyard. Around 1904 he added a sheep shed to the west, a poultry house to the south, and a fieldstone piggery to the east farther down the slope. The barnyard gave the cows sheltered access to the outdoors. All these buildings featured the abundant ventilation, natural light, and space that Burnett believed was crucial to healthy, productive livestock. Generous runs extended behind the chicken coops and piggery *(below)*, and in the warmer months, all the animals lived outdoors—the chickens in a large, triangular pen east of the barn complex near the road and the pigs, sheep, and cattle on the hillside above the farmhouses. Other buildings supporting the farm operation included a blacksmith shop/garage (by 1907), cobblestone smokehouse (1904), beehives, duck house, root cellar, slaughterhouse, springhouses, poultry coops and brood houses, and dog kennel. The concrete footings of a boar pen once located across the road from the machine shop are still visible.

## Animals

Santanoni livestock had to satisfy three requirements: they had to be attractive, productive, and able to tolerate the poor pasturage and northern climate. Guernseys, known for their high-quality milk and butter, dominated the Santanoni dairy herd by 1907, largely replacing the hardy Brown Swiss. Over the years, Blackfaced Highland, Southdown, and Shropshire sheep shared the pastureland, as Pruyn sought both good meat and wool for Anna's knitting. Black Berkshire pigs, Wyandotte chickens, iridescent French Carneau pigeons, "quackless" Brazilian ducks, and Guinea fowl made for a colorful farm scene. Draft horses stabled in the 1895 barn pulled wagons, plowed fields, and worked treadmill-powered equipment. Robert Pruyn took the quality of his livestock seriously; he kept meticulous breeding records and entered prize-winning cows in the county and state fairs.

## Pastures, Garden, and Related Structures

At its peak, the farm at Santanoni had almost 200 cleared acres extending from the gate lodge to about a half mile past the farm complex. Stone walls and crossbuck fences of woven wire and peeled poles separated the land into orchard, hayfield, pasture, and garden. A half-acre vegetable garden and small orchard were about 300 yards farther up the road to camp on the left. Across the road were asparagus and strawberry patches, and hayfields extended a bit farther down the road. Burnett's introduction of experimental concrete hot beds (today's cold frames) to start seedlings early made a bountiful garden possible by extending the growing season.

The last major renovation at the farm—the addition of standardized dairy equipment in the cow barn—occurred after World War I. This included steel pipe stanchions, metal-framed name placards at each stall identifying the cow by name and pertinent breeding history, and self-activated drinking bowls supplied with water via an underground pipe from a spring across the road. A cork brick floor provided soft footing for the cows' hooves.

*It seems that every time a cow had a "passage," my father was right there with a shovel and a water hose.*

—Rowena Ross Putnam, herdsman's daughter, 1987

## The People

Robert Pruyn encouraged a sense of ownership and pride in his farm staff. Stories abound about the dedication of the staff. How the gardener Charles Petoff *(left)* insisted on harvesting vegetables himself for the Pruyns' table to insure quality. How the herdsman George Ross cleaned the Guenseys' tails with bleach and water, then braided and brushed them out in preparation for a visit from Pruyn. How "farm boss" Lewis Kinne's serious demeanor belied the immense responsibility he had to guarantee that the quality of all farm products, from the smoked hams to the butter, met Pruyn's exacting standards.

*Courtesy Adirondack Architectural Heritage*

Isolated from Newcomb town life, the staff at Santanoni's farm formed its own community. Though farm work was backbreaking and certainly monotonous in its routine, the memories of former residents are tinged with nostalgia—of harvest-time corn roasts in the field, rides on the sugar beet wagon, sledding on the upper pasture, lively mealtime conversations with the bachelor farm hand boarders. Certain farm families spent one or even two decades as residents, so it is no surprise that their names have come to be associated with the farmhouses.

The herdsman's cottage, home to dairyman George Ross, his wife, Lettie, and daughter, Rowena, from about 1922 to 1931, incorporates the farmhouse (ca. 1850) present when Robert Pruyn purchased the farm parcels. Originally a simple, one-story, timber-framed structure, it was renovated as a Shingle Style bungalow. Three dormers were added and the roof was extended to create a front porch supported on peeled posts; interior beadboard finishes were added throughout. Caleb Chase, who cared for the draft horses, and Clifton Parker, a teamster, boarded with the family, as did various seasonal laborers hired to cut firewood or ice or tap the preserve's 900 maple trees.

The gardener's cottage, built around 1904 for the farm manager, later became the home of Bulgarian-born gardener Charles Petoff, his wife, Penna, their three children, and a nephew from 1919 to 1931. The shingle-clad house has typical rustic Adirondack detailing such as peeled cedar porch railings and eave brackets and deep roof overhangs.

*Courtesy Adirondack Museum*

Robert Pruyn probably ordered the last major farm building, the farm manager's house *(below)*, from a catalog around 1919. In the early decades of the 1900s, people could purchase house kits in a variety of styles from companies, including Sears, Roebuck and Harris Brothers. The house arrived by railroad boxcar with detailed plans and all the materials required to build it—the lumber, roofing and siding, as well as hardware, a furnace, and appliances. Farm manager Lewis Kinne, his wife, Minnie, and a niece occupied the house from 1919 until the farm closed in 1931. Art Tummins, the only employee retained after the farm closed, lived there with his wife, Helen, until the 1940s, when they moved to the West cottage near the gate lodge. Cobblestone masonry in the piers and porch parapets recalls the rustic stonework of other buildings on the preserve, but its clapboard sheathing differs from the shingles of the other buildings.

The stock market crash of 1929 and Robert Pruyn's declining health spelled the end for this beloved enterprise. Repairs to the buildings, fences, and roads, and the purchase of livestock and feed were costly. When the farm closed in 1931, some members of the farm community lost the only home they had ever known. The Melvin family, who purchased Santanoni in 1953, never used the farm. When the state of New York acquired the preserve in 1972, it demolished some of the buildings, severely deteriorated after 40 years of neglect.

*Lew and Minnie Kinne, 1922*
*Courtesy Adirondack Museum*

*Teamster Clifton Parker and Minnie Kinne*
*Courtesy Adirondack Museum*

I'd come home from school, drop my books, grab my [roller] skates and head for the barn. The floor was all [concrete]. I would skate back and forth between the two rows of cows for at least an hour. I can still see it now. I would skate in one direction and the cows would turn their heads to watch. When I came back the other way, they would turn their heads that way. Just like watching a tennis match. The barn had a silo, but it was never used. I used to go in there to hoot and holler and listen to my voice echo all over the place.

—Rowena Ross Putnam, herdsman's daughter, 1988

# The Road to the Main Camp

Over the 16 years it took Robert Pruyn to develop his estate, he continued to purchase land between Newcomb Lake and the village center, relocating residents along the old road and rebuilding it for his personal use, despite its status as a public way. Though no longer maintained by the town, hunters, anglers, and hikers used it to reach the lake. E.R. Wallace's 1895 edition of *Descriptive Guide to the Adirondacks* encouraged visitors to discover Lake Delia [Newcomb] by "a fine carriage road through a primeval forest." No doubt this advertisement about his private land bothered Pruyn. Eventually he convinced the town to cede rights to public access to the property along the old road.

Discovering traces of the history of Camp Santanoni along the road today requires a sharp eye. Gone is the low guardrail of peeled logs, designed by Ned Pruyn, which defined the edges of the road and provided seating for weary walkers. Cellar holes are all that remain of old farmsteads that Robert Pruyn removed. Hollowed-out borrow pits, where soil was excavated for road construction, are now overgrown with vegetation and blend into the forest. What little remains of the gardens, orchard, and hayfields is slowly returning to woodland. About two miles from the gate lodge is the Honeymoon Bridge, where Robert's young cousin, Huybertie Pruyn Hamlin, and her new husband stopped for photographs on their honeymoon at Santanoni in 1897, followed about a mile later by the Twin Bridges.

The 1893 New York State Forest Commission report described the entry road to Santanoni as "a well-graveled drive, smooth as a park road, affording a delightful ride through a grand old forest, with charming views here and there of the lofty mountains of the Marcy Range." Though Robert Pruyn prized the wildness of his preserve, he treated the roadway like an urban park, insisting that the edges where forest met road be raked clean of debris before the arrival of guests.

# The Service Complex

After three miles of tranquil passage through the woods, visitors rounded a bend to a bustling service complex that supported activities at the main camp. Hugging the southern shore of Newcomb Lake, the service complex was a self-contained enclave, with stable, garage, lodging, laundry, and icehouse. Constructed shortly after the main camp, it may have been the work of Robert Robertson, architect of the log villa. Like the rest of the preserve complexes, the buildings, with their dark-stained shingles and red trim, formed a cohesive visual group. Today, nothing remains of this once vibrant area of the preserve.

*Icehouse (left) and other service complex buildings from the lake*

A stable and a caretaker's house dominated the complex. The stable *(above left)* was built in 1893 as a simple, steeply gabled barn. A few years later, Edward Burnett oversaw its expansion, adding a 17 x 48-foot stable with seven stalls on the ground and a hayloft above. Large, sliding doors at either end accommodated carriages, wagons, and later, automobiles. A two-story addition facing the lake provided additional staff housing. Adjacent to the Duck Hole Bridge was the caretaker's house (ca. 1893, *opposite page, right*), a spacious, two-story, shingled building. Like other staff housing, it had running water but no electricity. Santanoni's caretakers wore many hats, serving as gamekeepers, guides, and handymen as the need arose. This was

*Courtesy Adirondack Architectural Heritage*

the main residence of "camp boss" Lester "Buster" Dunham and his family from 1921 until the layoff in 1931. It was probably the residence of Dunham's predecessors over the years, including Elbert Parker, Santanoni's first caretaker. Bachelor staff—handyman Vern Pelcher, chauffeur Ed Guy, and Art Tummins *(left)*, caretaker from 1931 until his retirement in 1976—boarded in the rear section of the house and ate meals with the family. The smaller chauffeur's house provided additional lodging for stablemen, chauffeurs, and other staff. A simple, one-story garage housed the Pruyn family's Lincoln limousine and other vehicles. It may have been the original carriage house for the service complex before the barn was expanded. Nearby stood a small laundry building with old-fashioned flat irons and tubs and stoves to heat wash water.

It required 35 bedrooms spread out over the four building complexes to house the sizable staff. For the butler, chef, chauffeur, and Mrs. Pruyn's personal maid, who traveled with the family from Albany, a trip to Santanoni was a working vacation. Since guests spent much of the time outdoors, there was only light housework and a more relaxed atmosphere. Staff could socialize in a screened recreation pavilion behind the kitchen wing or enjoy swimming and boating at the service complex. The rest of the year-round and seasonal staff came from Newcomb or neighboring communities. Santanoni staff was expected to create an illusion of rusticity that allowed the Pruyns and their guests to adventure in the wilderness but return to the formal rituals of upper class life.

> *When the gang was coming up from New York in the autumn, [Buster Dunham's wife, Nellie] had to do a lot of baking—maybe 24 or 25 pies—and the deer would smell the spice and they would come in and stick their heads right in the bake house, right in the window.*
>
> —Marion Dunham, family member, 1992

# Adirondack Rustic and the Japanese Influence

*There are only two attitudes toward nature.*
*One confronts it or one accepts it.*
—Teiji Itoh, Japanese garden scholar

The Adirondack rustic style of Great Camps like Santanoni is an American hybrid. Part Swiss chalet, part Japanese tea house, part log cabin, the style was uniquely suited to the northern climate. Stone footings raised the buildings off the ground to prevent water damage, massive roof timbers supported heavy snow loads, and deep roof overhangs protected buildings from ice and snow. Unlike its showy Gilded Age cousin, the 70-room "cottage" of Newport, Rhode Island, the Great Camp was designed to blend into its wilderness setting.

Initially developed in the 1870s by William West Durant, heir to a railroad fortune, the style was especially popular in the late 1800s and early 1900s for a wide range of building types. But it reached its zenith in its application to the Great Camps, family estates situated on remote lakes. Here the owners created compounds with separate buildings for separate uses—recreation, dining, library, lounging, and sleeping. In the early years, with limited access to food and other services, many camps functioned as self-sufficient communities with a farm, ice- and springhouses, smokehouse, sugarhouse, blacksmith, and other workshops. The use of locally sourced, rustic materials to harmonize with the setting—fieldstone and cobblestone for fireplaces, foundations and chimneys; exposed logs for porch railings and gable and eave details; bark siding; and sculptural branches and roots—sometimes was so extravagant as to have the opposite effect. Combined with the sheer number of buildings, the presence in the forest could be monumental.

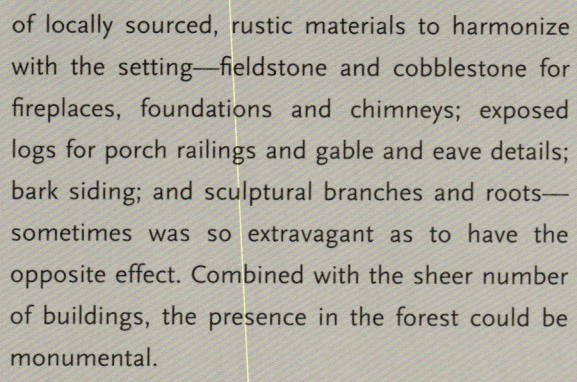

At Santanoni the rustic character was more understated, largely due to the influence of a Japanese aesthetic. The concept of shibui, meaning "tasteful in a rustic manner," is evident

*Photo Nina Caruso*

everywhere. The complexity of subtle details balances the overall simplicity of the building. The design employs decorative elements like peeled logs, fieldstone, birch bark, and split-log mosaic decoration with restraint. Likewise, the number of buildings was relatively modest, with dining and lounging sharing space in the main lodge and recreation on the broad veranda and at the boathouse.

But Santanoni's most unusual Japanese feature is not obvious. Seen from the air, the plan of the main camp assumes the form of a bird—the gable of the main lodge the head, the kitchen block the tail, the cabins stepped back like outstretched wings. This is the phoenix, a Buddhist icon, flying across the lake toward a western paradise, the vast wilderness of the Adirondacks.

From the ground, the impression is subtler. A single roof and a deep veranda connect six pavilions, blurring the distinction between indoor and outdoor space. The grand, central entrance of traditional architecture is absent. Here, the kitchen block is the first building visible from the informal entrance under the porte-cochère. Stepping onto the porch, the visitor must wander, at each turn entering another intimate outdoor room with a different view of the landscape. For the Pruyns, this was a place meant for contemplation.

In a letter to his wife from Japan, young Robert's father wrote, "I have lived in the open air all day, except when at meals. Sometimes I write on the piazza. Indeed all the people live here out of their houses and I am getting to be thoroughly Japanese in this respect." (Kanagawa, Sept. 19 1862) Surely Santanoni's design responds to Robert Pruyn's adolescent memories of a life spent outdoors.

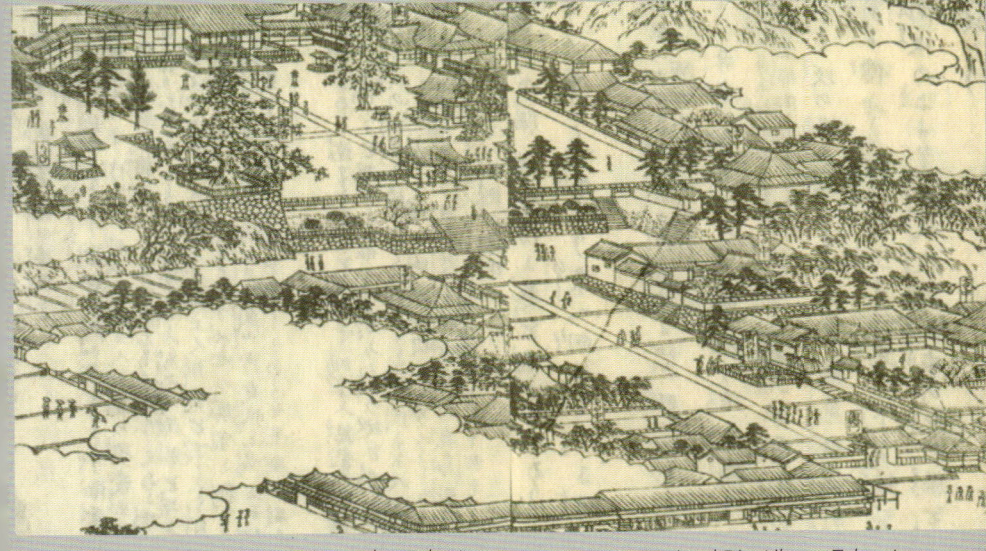

*Zempukugi Temple, U.S. Legation, Edo (Tokyo)*     *Courtesy National Diet Library, Tokyo, Japan*

# The Main Camp Complex

Main Lodge
Pump House
Artist's Studio
Boathouse
Kitchen/Service Wing
Gazebo
Generator Building
Icehouse Ruins
Wood Shed Site
Ash House
Workshop Ruins

Service Complex

Site
Ruins
Existing

N

*People generally like the unique simplicity, the strange difference from the ordinary country place, the ease of living and freedom from care. You have all the requirements of comfortable living without the jostling of the crowd or the tyranny of conventional life. . . . The world is at arm's length and nature is your intimate.*

—Robert C. Pruyn, 1915

Newcomb Lake

Bathhouse

The informal entrance to the log villa

Like a woodland creature, the villa at Camp Santanoni hides in low-growing, forest scrub. Screened from the lake by shoreline trees, its dark brown-stained logs blend into the landscape. It is solid, powerful, but not ostentatious. Stepping onto a porch obscured by a rocky outcropping and following it around several corners, it is possible to glimpse slivers of lake through the trees. But the full impact of its location is only apparent from the shore, which offers a sweeping vista of a wall of mountains, like a theater backdrop to pristine Newcomb Lake. To the north, solitary Santanoni Peak stands sentinel at the southern gateway to the High Peaks region of the Adirondacks. It is quiet, save the cry of loons.

Courtesy NYSDEC

## The Log Villa (1893)

Sixteen thousand square feet of roof, 5,000 square feet of porch, 1,500 spruce trees for the log walls—the numbers are staggering, and yet the villa's presence in the forest is relatively unobtrusive. Robert Robertson's *(above)* contribution as architect is certain, but what of the local laborers

Photo © Jane Riley

and craftsmen responsible for turning plans into reality? They had the craftsmanship to lay the stone for seven chimneys and nine fireplaces; the patience to finish and tightly set the log walls; the artistry to fabricate the mosaics of half-logs on doors and walls; the precision to lay a level floor on the variable contours of the site. Though their names are lost, Santanoni stands as a testament to their immense skill and pride of workmanship.

Dark and brooding, the initial impression of Santanoni is of its heavy massing. Nine-inch-diameter logs—peeled, then laid and chinked tightly with fibrous oakum and lime—form fortress-like walls. Throughout the buildings of the main camp, the delicacy of the red-trimmed windows stands in marked contrast to the heft of these log walls. Small panes of glass and narrow muntins mimic the airiness of a Japanese paper shoji screen.

At the center of the villa stood the main lodge, flanked by four cabins—two to the north and two to the south. The near north and south cabins contained two bedrooms, each with its own fieldstone fireplace, and a shared bathroom. The northernmost cabin was a single, large room with a stone fireplace; the southernmost cabin, originally of the same configuration, was enlarged later by enclosing the lakeside porch to create two rooms. Beadboard wainscoting and natural fiber wallcoverings added to the rustic charm.

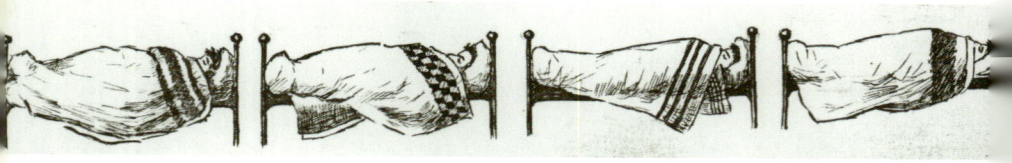

The simple plan of the four cabins reflected the Pruyns' expectation that visitors would spend most of their time on the porch or in the main lodge when they weren't exploring the preserve. Metal "backbreaker beds" with horsehair mattresses discouraged lingering in bed. And yet, in a letter to her mother during the first spring party at Santanoni in 1893, the irrepressible Bertie Pruyn wrote: "It is simply stunning here. You cannot imagine how elegant we are. Mabel, Bessie and I are in one huge room with a bath room—tub and all attached. Each a dear little iron bed, and lovely bureaus, washstands, curtains, and easy chairs—extremely luxurious in every way." Bright red and black Hudson Bay blankets and linens monogrammed with the camp name added homey touches to the décor.

The main lodge was the center of activity at Santanoni. A massive stone chimney with back-to-back fireplaces anchored the room at its center. A lounging area with couches and chairs occupied the front section of the room. Along the perimeter of this space, under a continuous band of windows, was a built-in bench with integrated storage. Another row of windows at ceiling height brought additional afternoon light into the dark room. Small, split logs arranged diagonally and vertically formed a seven-foot wainscot. Birch bark paneling on the upper wall and ceiling reflected light to brighten the room. The rear half of the room contained a library and game area on the left by the stairway and a dining area to the right. Here Japanese tatami (grass) mats decorated the wall above a split log wainscot. Matched, bark-covered tree trunks form the balusters for the stairway *(below)*, providing a semi-transparent screen between the living area and the stairs to guest rooms. From the back of the main lodge, a small hallway led to a butler's pantry on the right. A spring room on the left contained a large, lead-lined cistern to collect drinking water. The gravity-fed system drew water from a spring across the lake.

Photo © Jane Riley

Exiting the back hall, the staff crossed a covered walkway to the kitchen block. Here two wood cookstoves, joined by a gas one later, produced meals as elaborate as those served in Albany, with food fresh from the farm. A door from the back of the kitchen led onto a second-story porch with broad steps to the ground for easy access to service buildings. Built-in ice chests and a walk-in meat cooler, a linen room, and a fishing tackle room provided storage space to supplement two large pantries off the main kitchen. Seven staff bedrooms and a bathroom occupied the top floor. Beneath the building were a double-walled, stone wine cellar, vegetable cellar, and wood shed. The back porch of the kitchen *(above)* was a hub of activity for staff and guests. Here fishing parties unloaded the day's catch and the gardener delivered produce. Rock salt discarded near the porch from the hand-cranked ice cream maker attracted deer to the stairs—and not far behind them, the children, who took great delight in taming "Harriet" the doe to eat saltines out of their hands.

Unlike many of the Great Camps, where custom-built, rustic furniture completed the décor, the interiors at Santanoni contained mass-produced, Victorian and Mission style furniture popular at the time, interspersed with Japanese collectibles. Lamps with pleated shades, porcelain vases, and a screen between the library and dining area made no pretense of blending with the rustic architecture. A large antique Japanese temple gong on the front porch called everyone to meals.

The expansive veranda of the main camp functioned as an outdoor living space. To improve ventilation and light, the gables of the villa were left open to expose a decorative truss system. The deep, angled veranda offered shelter from inclement weather, intimate space for quiet pastimes like reading and games, and room for activities like dancing or Ping-Pong. On rainy days, Anna Pruyn was said to walk the full length of the porch 20 times for a mile of exercise.

Flanking the villa at its northern edge was the artist's studio (ca. 1905; *below*), designed by Delano and Aldrich for the Pruyns' eldest son, Ned, *(left)*, whose watercolors and etchings chronicle life at Santanoni. Its log walls and rubble foundation blend with the log villa, while a fieldstone gable incorporating an arched window recalls the stone arches of the gate lodge and creamery. A fieldstone chimney seems to emerge from the massive boulder on which it rests. A fieldstone fireplace, exposed beams, and natural fiber wallcoverings enhance the rusticity of the interior. A high ceiling and northern light make this an ideal studio. Perched on a knoll near the studio was daughter Ruth's refuge, a red-painted, cedar post and screen gazebo. The current one is a reconstruction for the Melvin grandchildren. About a quarter mile farther down the shore were a sandy beach and a shingled bathhouse with four changing rooms.

Balancing the complex at the southern edge of the camp was the boathouse (ca. 1895; *below*). Family photo albums attest to the vital role this building played in the life of the camp. The cavernous log building had two boat slips and a broad center ramp for hauling lighter boats into the boathouse. The Pruyns had a variety of guideboats, skiffs, and two elegant sailing canoes, one now in the collection of the Adirondack Museum in Blue Mountain Lake. Sequestered in a cove sheltered by Little Minister Island, the boathouse was the launch site for many an outing. Two floating pine logs, one still visible next to the ramp, acted as breakwaters between the island and the boathouse.

Scattered behind the kitchen block were several support structures, including: a small, shingled generator building (ca. 1935) erected to shelter the new Kohler generator; an unpeeled spruce log icehouse (ca. 1892); a fieldstone ash house (ca. 1900) for the storage of fuel for lamps and the generator; and an old workshop (ca. 1900). On the shoreline in front of the main lodge stood a pump house (ca. 1900), sheathed in cedar bark. When water in the attic tank fell below a certain level, the pump drew lake water for washing, plumbing, and fire protection.

## Camp Life

Life at Santanoni was as understated as its architecture. A typical weekend guest list included about 15 family members and close friends, a small group compared to the large gatherings at other Great Camps. This was a place for connecting with nature, not the rich and famous.

Robert Pruyn's private preserve had a wealth of natural features readily accessible to visitors. In addition to the delights of Newcomb Lake, with its seven islands to explore, excellent fishing, and a sandy beach for swimming just minutes from the camp, there were 15 miles of well-maintained hiking trails and four other ponds. A trip to the largest, Moose Pond, was a favorite. Here a lean-to and boathouse set the stage for elaborate picnics. And, of course, a visit to Robert Pruyn's model farm to admire the livestock and gardens was a must. Whatever the adventure, guests could expect the attention of a discreet service staff. After a long day outdoors, they would enjoy a hot bath in a cabin warmed by a fire. Dirty clothes were washed, pressed, and returned the next day; muddy shoes and boots left outside a cabin door at night reappeared polished the next morning.

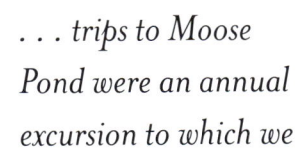

> . . . trips to Moose Pond were an annual excursion to which we all looked forward, and we rowed and fished from a boat kept there in a locked boathouse and where were also stored kettles and other necessaries for a most galumptious repast cooked by the guides over a camp fire. Forked sticks held the trout if any had been caught in time, and the most delicious frizzled bacon accompanied them.
>
> —Huybertie Pruyn, *The Four Spring Parties to Santanoni*

Over 40 years of guest books, journals, and scrapbooks bring Santanoni to life. The annual spring fishing party opened the season. Men and women alike embraced this popular sport. The Pruyns stocked the lake with trout and used fish weirs and pisciculture to improve the stock. A camp journal titled, "Santanoni: Record of Fish and of Some Other Things," documented various activities, the weather, and above all, fishing in detail—the total catch, the size, the weather conditions, type of lure, who caught what, and where. Wildlife encounters, related with the relish and enthusiasm of hindsight, included mountain lion, bear, fox, porcupine, mice, and deer.

> *Clear. Water 46 degrees, air 45 degrees, 7 a.m. Gov. and Mrs. Roosevelt left. Mr. and Mrs. Elkins and Mr. and Mrs. Richmond arrived. Seven trout.*
>
> —Camp Journal, May 22, 1899

"Bits of Fact and Fiction By All," a light-hearted scrapbook compiled by family and visitors, reveals the loosening of the Gilded Age social regimen at Santanoni. Bertie Pruyn recalls that the hijinks of the young infected a more staid older generation: "There was a mania for practical jokes—even the elders partook of this mania, and we felt encouraged when they thought of something to perpetrate on some older victim." Nevertheless, the elders tried to limit improprieties by separating the living quarters of the single men and women by 250 feet of porch. The distant cabins acquired the names of two monsters separated by a treacherous channel in Homer's *Odyssey*: the far north was "Charybdis" (the whirlpool), for the men and the far south was "Scylla" (the sea monster), for the women. In spite of these efforts to monitor contact, tales of their flirtations and antics abound.

*Cora, Fred and I climbed a ladder and with a big lake trout slipping around in Fred's hands, attached him with wire and string and let him down the chimney of the Bowditch's room, so when they went to bed they found a nice trout slowly cooking for a midnight supper. I suppose we considered that very clever.*

—Huybertie Pruyn, *The Four Spring Parties to Santanoni*

But it was, after all, the Gilded Age, and social propriety was everything to the privileged class. Female visitors had to find ways to adapt the strict dress code to the rigors of outdoor recreation. The results were far from fashionable—heavy skirts and sweaters that Bertie Pruyn *(far right)* remembered felt "like armor . . . and then came the hat question—it never occurred to us to do without them. Mabel had a very becoming tricorne while Bessie had a squash felt with her fish flies caught around the hat band, and I had an orange felt called a 'Land and water hat' presumably because it was good for any time or place." Dinner was a lengthy, formal affair followed by reading aloud, composing poetry, music performed by guests or occasionally local talent, and charades. Special events like masquerade balls and rowing regattas inspired a playful, competitive spirit.

Remote though it was, Santanoni could not escape the passage of time. As the Pruyn children grew into adulthood with families of their own, the seasonal gatherings gave way to less formal visits. Anna and Robert began to use the cabin "Scylla" as their quarters. Close to the lake and boathouse, it was a manageable size for their simpler needs.

After Robert's death in 1934, Anna continued to visit Santanoni until her death in 1939. In the following decades, the Pruyn descendants continued to honor the spirit of rustic simplicity they valued so deeply. Ice was harvested from the lake into the 1940s although refrigeration was available; a single generator provided limited illumination to camp buildings even after electricity was an option.

*Ned Pruyn and wife, Erick, with children Susan and Lance and a family friend, circa 1948*

Robert and Anna's children shared their love of Santanoni with their own children. Granddaughter Susan Pruyn King recalls, "While Dad [Ned Pruyn] was alive, he taught us as much as he could about the woods. Most of all, he tried to instill common sense . . . to always think first before any action there, to never, never underestimate Nature, to respect that Nature knows a great deal more than Man will ever know. Having given us this basis, he allowed us a great deal of freedom." And so idyllic summer days passed for a new generation—exploring the lake and woods, fishing, collecting plants to create "forest gardens" on kitchen platters as Anna had taught her children, and inventing their own games. "Most of the very best of me comes from Santanoni, the memories and what I learned there," says Susan.

*Painting by Edward Lansing Pruyn*

## The Melvin Years

Two World Wars and the Great Depression altered the complexion of American society. When Syracuse brothers Myron and Crandall Melvin purchased Camp Santanoni in 1953, the type of wealth and privilege of the Pruyns' world largely was gone, diluted by a large middle class demanding political and social equality. Progressive where the Pruyns were conservative, the Melvins attended public school, followed by Syracuse University for both college and law school. The brothers established a successful law practice in 1921. Crandall eventually became president, and later chairman, of Merchants' National Bank and Trust Company, where he developed credit and loan programs to assist farmers and businessmen after the Depression.

*Courtesy NYSDEC*

The camp buildings at Santanoni must have seemed as exotic to the Melvins as they do to visitors today. However, 20 years of deferred maintenance during management of the preserve by the Robert C. Pruyn Trust left the property in poor condition. Rather than demolish the deteriorated buildings, the Melvins rolled up their shirtsleeves and brought their Yankee work ethic to bear at Santanoni. By painting and reroofing, they saved many of these buildings from ruin. Thanks to an approach that covered up, rather than removed, existing building materials, much of the original detail at Santanoni survived under wallboard and ceiling and floor tiles. The removal of a portion of the stone wall near the gate lodge, which allowed logging trucks to enter without navigating the stone arch, was perhaps the most significant alteration during their ownership.

The disappearance of Myron Melvin's young grandson Douglas Legg in 1971 opened up the preserve to the public for the first time in 80 years. More than 1,000 volunteers—some local, others from beyond the region—combed the preserve for over a month without success. The dedication of the town to the search reminded residents of a history shared with Camp Santanoni.

## Journey to Preservation and Protection

*Student Conservation Association interns reshingle the gate lodge boathouse, summer 2012. Courtesy NYSDEC*

The Santanoni Preserve has been a crucible for an age-old debate over the co-existence of man and nature. The Great Camp's journey from the brink of loss to National Historic Landmark status has been a long one; it took more than 25 years of complex negotiation between the state and local government, environmental and historic preservation organizations, and citizens before Santanoni received legal protection. Even now, its status as a "Historic Area" within the Adirondack Forest Preserve presents both challenges and opportunities. Thanks to Forest Preserve protection, it remains remarkably intact in its wilderness setting. At the same time, state regulations may limit the ability to repair and restore buildings, maintain the surrounding landscape that provides a context for their meaning, and interpret the site to the public.

After several failed attempts in the late 1950s and the 1960s by the Melvin family and the state of New York to reach agreement on the sale of the Santanoni Preserve, the introduction of a third party, the Nature Conservancy—a national land conservation nonprofit organization—opened a new door. Working in tandem with the state and other interest groups, the newly created Adirondack chapter of the Nature Conservancy brokered a land transfer agreement with the Melvins that closed on February 18, 1972. This placed the property under the jurisdiction of the state's Department of Environmental Conservation (DEC).

The future of the historic buildings on the Santanoni Preserve hung in limbo for almost 20 more years because of the ongoing controversy about how to resolve the existence of these buildings under the "forever wild" strictures of the Forest Preserve. In most instances, the DEC removes all buildings—historic or modern—on Forest Preserve land to return it to wilderness; during its early ownership, the DEC did demolish all the buildings at the service complex and the most severely deteriorated ones at the farm.

In the 1970s and 1980s, a growing appreciation for the Great Camp as a regional building type drew attention to the historic buildings at Santanoni. Enthusiasm for Santanoni grew as visitors, making the five-mile hike or bicycle ride into the main camp, increasingly fell under its spell. In 1990 preservationist Howard Kirschenbaum spearheaded the creation of Adirondack Architectural Heritage (AARCH), a nonprofit historic preservation education and advocacy organization for the Adirondack Park.

*AARCH Director Steven Engelhart leads a tour of the main camp.*

The preservation of Camp Santanoni would be its first major advocacy project. The town of Newcomb, under the leadership of its supervisor George Canon, provided additional key support for preservation of the camp as both an important chapter in local history and as a tourist attraction that would benefit the local economy.

AARCH raised public awareness about the historic and architectural importance of Santanoni in a variety ways. It staffed it with summer interpreters, offered day-long public tours of the camp, publicized it through media coverage and public lectures, and produced a free guide to the site. The publication of *Santanoni: From Japanese Temple to Life at an Adirondack Great Camp* in 2000 was the culmination of over a decade of research by authors Robert Engel, Howard Kirschenbaum, and Paul Malo. Preservation consultant Wesley Haynes, DEC Historic Preservation Officer J. Winthrop Aldrich, and Pruyn family members contributed significantly to the research.

*Howard Kirschenbaum (left) and DEC Preservation Officer Charles Vandrei on main lodge roof*

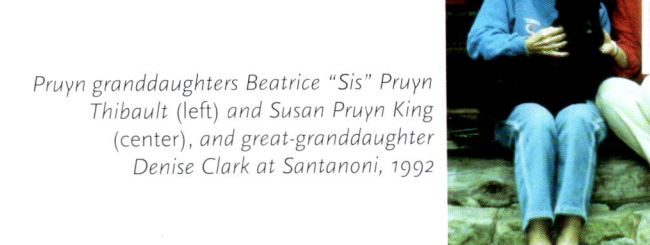

*Pruyn granddaughters Beatrice "Sis" Pruyn Thibault (left) and Susan Pruyn King (center), and great-granddaughter Denise Clark at Santanoni, 1992*

At the same time, AARCH and the DEC pulled together a coalition of environmental, historic preservation, and local groups to reach consensus on a legal solution that would permit Santanoni's preservation and public use within the framework of the Adirondack State Land Master Plan. DEC Historic Preservation Officer Charles Vandrei played a key role in the agency's unit management planning process.

The dedication of the Santanoni partnership paid off in 2000 with three significant events that would do much to safeguard its future: The National Park Service designated Santanoni a National Historic Landmark and the Adirondack Park Agency approved both its reclassification as "historic" under the State Land Master Plan and the DEC's unit management plan for the site.

Meanwhile, the state and AARCH undertook critical building stabilization and exterior restoration work to halt further decay. The partnership used funding from several state agencies, the federal Save America's Treasures program, the town of Newcomb, and donations from Friends of Camp Santanoni to replace roofs, fix major structural problems, and restore porches and other exterior elements. Two architectural firms—Crawford and Stearns of Syracuse and Argus Architecture and Preservation of Troy—prepared a site-wide conservation plan in 2003 and guided some of the larger restoration projects. By 2012 the partners had collectively completed more than $1.7 million in work on 17 buildings, but a tragic fire that destroyed the barn complex in 2004 was a reminder of the tenuous nature of this historic site and the importance of developing better fire protection for the vulnerable wooden buildings.

In 1997 the Santanoni partnership brought master craftsman Michael Frenette *(left)* of Tupper Lake into the restoration process. Recently returned from a training program in wood preservation technology sponsored by the International Council on Monuments and Sites (ICOMOS) in Norway, he was a perfect fit for the job. In addition to his training, he had enjoyed several summers as a New York State backcountry ranger in the Adirondacks. Other than the replacement of the roof and structural stabilization of the kitchen wing, he has worked on nearly every building at the main camp, from restoration of the porch and complete reconstruction of the collapsed boathouse to restoration and repair of every other outbuilding. He has supervised interns and volunteer crews on projects that include replacement of several roofs, repair of the main porch and windows, and staining of the main camp walls and porch.

Today, through an Adopt-A-Natural Resource agreement with the DEC, AARCH has many responsibilities at the site. Led by Executive Director Steven Engelhart, it develops the annual work plan, hires and trains seasonal staff, advocates and raises funds for its preservation, and oversees restoration projects with generous financial support from the town of Newcomb. Project funding and execution vary, reflecting the complex nature of ownership and management. Depending on the project, a general contractor, DEC crew, Michael Frenette, volunteers, or a combination of these, may complete the work. For example, the DEC has completed most of the work at the farm, while general contractor Mercer Construction Company of Albany performed exterior conservation and structural work at the gate lodge and West cottage.

Michael Frenette understands the uncanny spell that Santanoni casts over visitors. For 15 summers he has lived at the camp without electricity or running water, chilling his food with a block of ice and hauling lake water to a small tub for washing. He marvels at the log villa's brilliant design and siting that circulate breezes along the porch, fending off bugs and summer's heat. In the afternoons, he invites volunteers, interns, and friends to share tea—served in delicate porcelain cups—honoring the Pruyns' spirit of hospitality and rustic simplicity.

*Photo © Jane Riley*

*Photos in this section
courtesy Adirondack Architectural Heritage
unless otherwise noted*

## A Timeless Quest

"The great question, whether man is of nature or above her," wrote pioneering conservationist George Perkins Marsh in his seminal work, *Man and Nature* (1864). His examination of the environmental consequences of deforestation strengthened support for the establishment of the Adirondack Park in 1892. At the heart of this centuries-old debate about man's place in the natural world was this: Did nature exist solely for man's use and benefit, or did man have a responsibility to minimize his impact and live in harmony with nature?

This complex relationship between man and nature played out on a smaller stage at Camp Santanoni. In its design and use, the Pruyns sought a romantic expression of wilderness, unspoiled by exploitation or modern intrusions. Yet the tension between wilderness and civilization is present in the co-existence of the gate lodge, farm, and log villa within their wild setting. The formal gate lodge at the preserve entrance proudly announced to visitors that this was an estate shaped by human hands. And while the villa deferred to nature in its use of natural materials and integration with the landscape, the 200-acre farm represented years of effort to tame a rugged landscape poorly suited for agriculture. Though the Pruyns and their guests ventured into the wilderness, they returned each evening to the trappings of civilized life.

Camp Santanoni was a product of the Gilded Age, a period of rapid industrialization and economic growth that placed enormous wealth in the hands of a few. The exodus of rural dwellers for job opportunities in the city radically altered the agrarian way of life, severing the traditional relationship between people and the land. Yet some byproducts of urbanization—poverty, pollution, crime, disease—convinced many that America had lost its soul in the name of progress. The romantic depiction of nature by writers and artists in the mid and late 1800s reawakened a yearning in Americans to reconnect to wild land as the embodiment of truth, beauty, and freedom.

Life in the digital age sets up a similar dynamic. Technological advances like computers and cell phones may connect us, but they also isolate us. It is possible to conduct business, socialize, and shop without stepping outdoors or hearing a human voice. Perhaps this is why Santanoni's story has become our own, as we search for a way to reconnect with nature and, in so doing, with each other.

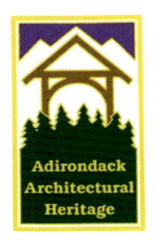

Adirondack Architectural Heritage (AARCH) is the private non-profit, historic preservation organization for the Adirondack region of New York State. Its mission is to further better public understanding, appreciation, and stewardship of the region's architecture, historic sites, and communities. AARCH fulfills this mission through its educational programs, advocacy, technical assistance, and partnerships with others.

For more information about AARCH, visit our web site at www.aarch.org, contact us at 1745 Main Street, Keeseville, NY 12944, or call (518) 834-9328.

AARCH manages Camp Santanoni with the New York State Department of Environmental Conservation through an Adopt-A-Natural Resource Agreement. The town of Newcomb is also a key player in this partnership and regularly provides funding for our collaborative planning, conservation, and interpretive work there. Hundreds of people support the preservation of Santanoni through the Friends of Camp Santanoni. For more about the Friends, visit: www.aarch.org/santanoni/help.

We would like to thank the following individuals and organizations for their assistance with this publication: Ted Comstock; Susan Pruyn King; Howard Kirschenbaum; Douglas McCombs and Erika Sanger, Albany Institute of History and Art; Angela Snye, Adirondack Museum; and Charles Vandrei, New York State Department of Environmental Conservation.

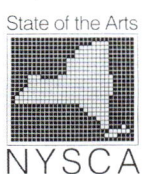

The Champlain Valley National Heritage Partnership and the town of Newcomb provided financial support for this publication. Much of AARCH's good work is made possible, in part, through the generous support of the New York State Council on the Arts, Architecture, Planning, and Design Program.

This project was funded by an agreement awarded by the United States National Park Service (NPS) to the New England Interstate Water Pollution Control Commission in partnership with the Champlain Valley National Heritage Partnership. NEIWPCC manages CVNHP's personnel, contract, grant, and budget tasks and provides input on the program's activities. The viewpoints expressed here do not necessarily represent those of NEIWPCC, CVNHP, LCBP or NPS, nor does mention of trade names, commercial products, or causes constitute endorsement or recommendation for use.

All photos are courtesy Susan Pruyn King, unless otherwise noted.

Several written resources were used in the preparation of this guidebook, chief among them, *Santanoni: From Japanese Temple to Life at an Adirondack Great Camp* by Robert Engel, Howard Kirschenbaum, and Paul Malo (Adirondack Architectural Heritage, 2009). Also helpful were: *Farm Complex and Gate Lodge Historic Structure Reports* (Wesley Haynes); *Edward Burnett: An Agricultural Designer on Gentlemen's Estates* (Taya Dixon); and *Santanoni Preserve Source Book #1* (J. Winthrop Aldrich).

Camp Santanoni resonates with visitors for many reasons. Some are intrigued by the Japanese-inspired architecture of its great log villa. Others are fascinated by the lifestyle at an Adirondack Great Camp or by a farm operation that produced an abundance and variety of food. Still others return, year after year, to admire each new accomplishment in our restoration work. But what almost everyone recalls is something less tangible, born of Santanoni's wild and magical setting on Newcomb Lake, surrounded by deep woods and mountains. It is a reminder that, yes, there is a way for humans and nature to be in balance.

Taking up the cause of the preservation of Camp Santanoni in 1990 was Adirondack Architectural Heritage's (AARCH) first major advocacy effort, one that bore fruit in 2000 when the state reclassified the site as "historic" and adopted a management plan for its preservation and public use. Today, AARCH has an active management role and a productive working relationship with the New York State Department of Environmental Conservation and the Town of Newcomb, which has provided invaluable long-term support for our efforts. Together the Santanoni team works to ensure that this remarkable site is renowned, enjoyed, and cherished.

Steven Engelhart, *Executive Director*
Adirondack Architectural Heritage